Cryptocurrency

and

Bitcoin

KENNY EVANS

Contents

CHAPTER 01

Introduction

A remarkable attention has acquired by Bitcoin and other prominent cryptocurrencies since the last several years. Around the world it is known as digital coin and virtual currency, is gained and traded within the blockchain framework. This innovation (blockchain technology) implemented in using the cryptocurrency has raised the eyebrows within the banking sector, government, stakeholders and individual investors. Cryptocurrency market has advanced capriciously and at unprecedented speed over the course of its short lifespan. Since the release of the pioneer anarchic cryptocurrency, Bitcoin, to the public in January 2009, more than 550 cryptocurrencies have been developed, the majority with only a modicum of success[1]. Research on the industry is still scarce. The majority of it is singularly focused on Bitcoin rather than a more diverse spread of cryptocurrencies and is gradually being outpaced by fluid industry developments, including new coins, technological progression, and increasing government regulation of the markets. However, the fluidity of the industry does, admittedly, present a challenge to research, a thorough evaluation of the cryptocurrency industry writ large is required. This paper seeks to provide a concise yet comprehensive analysis of the cryptocurrency industry with precise analysis of Bitcoin, the first decentralized cryptocurrency. Particular attention will be given to examining theoretical economic differences between existing coins.

It was first introduced by[2], an anonymous group or individual that has introduced Bitcoin as the first digital currency for easier day-to-day transaction from individual to individual. Bitcoin is operated without the middle man such as banks and monetary institutions. It is a form of peer-to-peer transaction, without the need to reveal one's identity for a transaction to happen. Unlike the current practice, the bank functions as the middleman or the go-between, knows the identity of buyer and seller, thus engendering the issues of personal data protection. Bitcoin platform has made the trading and transaction of cryptocurrency much easier and more independent, without compromising personal information and details. To some, opting for this method of transaction has entitled them to transact freely and anonymously. Bitcoin is the first digital coin in the world to have used the blockchain platform. It is created within a transaction log with computers participated across a network[3]. This blockchain has one of the highest security systems by not allowing fraudsters to use the currency more than once. The blockchain protocol rely on proof of work where it ensures miners converge to this structure. The computational operation is known as hashing where the term hashing power refers to the computational power of mining the currencies[4].

Bit of a History

Although the concept of electronic currency dates back to the late 1980s, Bitcoin, launched in 2009 by pseudonymous (and still unidentified) developer [2], is the first successful decentralized cryptocurrency [5]. In short, a cryptocurrency is a virtual coinage system that functions much like a standard currency, enabling users to provide virtual payment for goods and services free of a central trusted authority. Cryptocurrencies rely on the transmission of digital information, utilizing cryptographic methods to ensure legitimate, unique transactions. Bitcoin took the digital coin market one step further, decentralizing the currency and freeing it from hierarchical power structures. Instead, individuals and businesses transact with the coin electronically on a peer-to-peer network. It caught wide attention beginning in 2011, and various altcoins – a general name for all other cryptocurrencies post-Bitcoin – soon appeared. Litecoin was released in the fall of 2011, gaining modest success and enjoying the highest cryptocurrency market cap after Bitcoin until it was overtaken by Ripple on October 4th, 2014. Litecoin modified Bitcoin's protocol, increasing transaction speed with the idea that it would be more appropriate for day-to-day transactions. Ripple, launched in 2013, introduced an entirely unique model to that used by Bitcoin and currently maintains the second highest market capitalization of approximately $255 million (April 22) [6] [7]. Another notable coin in the evolutionary chain of cryptocurrency, Peercoin, employs a revolutionary technological development to secure and sustain its coinage [8]. Peercoin merges the PoW technology used by Bitcoin and Litecoin along with its own mechanism, proof-of-stake (PoS), to employ a hybrid network security mechanism. More recently NuShares/NuBits have emerged, introduced in August 2014, which rely on a dual currency model almost entirely divorced from the single currency model used by previous coins[9]. At the time this paper was written, the cryptocurrency industry consisted of over 550 coins with varying user bases and trade volumes [10]. Because of high volatility, the market capitalization of the cryptocurrency industry changes dramatically, but is estimated at the time of this paper to be just over $3.5 billion, with Bitcoin representing approximately 88% of the market cap [6].

The big question that arise as Bitcoin was introduced, are these cryptocurrencies considered as real money? According to [1], the history has outlined that money must have the following criteria:

i.   A store of value (purchasing power that users can manipulate to buy goods in the current time to the future).

ii.   A medium of exchange (ability to make payments).

iii.   A unit of account (value that can be measured of any goods for sale).

Money theoretically must meet all these criteria but it is not always the case. Analyzing Bitcoin and other cryptocurrency in their current form, all the three criteria are debatable. One can postulate that it does have a store value due to the ability for purchasing power, but due to uncertainty, one cannot estimate whether Bitcoin can be used in the future as it is being used now. For medium of exchange, some can justify that cryptocurrency can be used for a medium of exchange, but to others the goods that can be exchanged are limited.

If all these three criteria are set to be the pre-requirement for any commodity to be given the stature of money, therefore it should be accepted within the context of its use and application. [11] reported that cigarettes met all these criteria during the hard time of World

War II where prisoners in war camps used it for transaction. As for cryptocurrency, it can be regarded as money to people who are computer and internet enabled. The problem lies on the fact that only a small fraction of the people worldwide has the access to internet devices. Therefore, within this context, similar to the prisoner in the war camp, cryptocurrency only is limited to those having access to the internet. [1] reported that only about 20,000 Bitcoin holders in the United Kingdom with only 300 transactions each day. This number would be even smaller in emerging and developing countries due to the lack of internet access.

Primitively Was Bitcoin

Bitcoin is an open source, peer-to-peer digital currency first proposed in 2008, a white paper published under the name of S. Nakamoto. He begins his paper by stating that *"Commerce on the Internet has come to rely almost exclusively on financial institutions serving as trusted third parties to process electronic payments. While the system works well enough for most transactions, it still suffers from the inherent weakness of the trust based model"* [12].

Further, the existence of a trusted intermediary increases transaction costs, "cutting off the possibility for small casual transactions." Additionally, the trusted intermediaries are pressured to gather as much information about the parties as possible in order to control transaction costs. Therefore, [2] sought to create a coin that completely removed any trusted central authority and replace trust with cryptographic proof. This system would have the added benefits of having low transaction fees, low latency (time to make transactions), and pseudo-anonymity.

A bitcoin, and every subsequent cryptocurrency, is merely "a chain of digital signatures" where "Each owner transfers the coin to the next by digitally signing a hash of the previous transaction and the public key of the next owner and adding these to the end of the coin" so that ownership can dynamically be programmed into the coin [10]. Further, these lines of computer code are stored in a program called a "wallet" on personal hard drives and/or via online wallets like Coinbase. Like cash or commodities, bitcoins can be lost, stolen or destroyed. One British man became famous for throwing out his hard drive, and with it his wallet containing over 7,000 BTC, which had a market value of approximately $7 million at the time [13]. The prominent Bitcoin exchange, Mt. Gox, had nearly $350 million worth of bitcoin stolen in February 2014, forcing the exchange to declare bankruptcy and highlighting security issues within the cryptocurrency world[14].

Bitcoins can only be sent or received by logging the transaction on the public ledger, also known as the "blockchain." Bitcoins lack intrinsic value; rather, Bitcoin's value is purely a function of supply and demand [15]. Unlike paper "fiat currency" that derives value from a government, Bitcoin is neither created by, nor backed by, any government. Bitcoin protocol seeks to solve the double-spending problem (essentially, spending the same coin more than once) inherent in non-cash payment systems resulting in the need for a trusted third party (such as a bank or credit card company) to verify the integrity of the transaction. Double-spending occurs when an asset is duplicated, and thus can be spent multiple times. This problem does not exist in physical currencies, since transactions involve changing possession of property. However, a digital file has the potential to be copied. The security of cryptocurrency, however, and its ability to safeguard against such digital copying, is inherent in its blockchain or public ledger systems. These systems keep records of ownership and transaction timestamps, eliminating the possibility of digital copying and, thus, double-spending. The transaction at this point is considered complete, and ownership of the coin has been absolutely transferred, without fear of double-spending, because the entire network becomes informed of which wallet the coin currently resides in. Bitcoin was introduced to the public on January 3rd, 2009, but traded for less than a dollar until February 2011 [10]. Bitcoin reached an all-time high of $1151/coin on December 4th, 2013, and has since steadily declined. Despite this decline, it is apparent that daily trading volume has held steady for the past year.

Mining System

How was cryptocurrency initially received or gained? As to fiat money, it is issued by the central bank, while cryptocurrency is created by mining via the blockchain using cryptography technology. It is the method of issuing new cryptocurrency. The blockchain system comprising of developers, users, miners, node maintainers and the interactions that guarantee the functionality of distributed ledgers[16]. Such mining process requires miners to have capital expenses in purchasing the software and hardware. The software includes CGminer, GUIminer and BFGminer are the models used in Bitcoin mining[17]. While the hardware's are Avalon, AntMiner and ASICMiner. Mining of other currencies that uses many different algorithm requires the use of high-end and high-speed graphic cards. For a new miner, one needs to register a wallet and an encrypted banking online that can store and accept the cryptocurrency [17]. When a miner is able to solve the puzzle in the blockchain system, the digital coins will be rewarded and transferred to the wallet that has been predetermined earlier. According to many of the cryptocurrency protocols, the way mining works is by validating transaction by linking to the block that was accepted earlier[18]. Miners would have to solve the puzzle embedded in the block, which contain the hash of the previous block, the current block transaction hash and address that will be rewarded after the puzzle is solved. This is the basic of the mining process. This in turn created a block chain, a trace of the transaction that happened.

CHAPTER 02

Types of Cryptocurrency

According to coinmarketcap.com, at this time there are more than 550 diverse cryptocurrencies exist [19]. As the most important crypto currency, bitcoin has we discussed earlier. Now we are going to discuss Altcoins. What Are Altcoins?

Altcoins are alternatives to Bitcoin. They are cryptocurrencies that use a technology called blockchain that allows secure peer-to-peer transactions. [20] Altcoins build on the success of Bitcoin by slightly changing the rules to appeal to different users. Here's a list of cryptocurrency types representing the most popular industry crypto projects (at present):

Bitcoin Cash

Bitcoin Cash (BCH) holds an important place in the history of altcoins because it is one of the earliest and most successful hard forks of the original Bitcoin. In the cryptocurrency world, a fork takes place as the result of debates and arguments between developers and miners. Due to the decentralized nature of digital currencies, wholesale changes to the code underlying the token or coin at hand must be made due to general consensus; the mechanism for this process varies according to the particular cryptocurrency.

BCH began its life in August of 2017 as a result of one of these splits. The debate that led to the creation of BCH had to do with the issue of scalability; the Bitcoin network has a limit on the size of blocks: one megabyte (MB). BCH increases the block size from one MB to eight MB, with the idea being that larger blocks can hold more transactions within them, and therefore the transaction speed would be increased. It also makes other changes, including the removal of the Segregated Witness protocol which impacts block space. As of January 2021, BCH had a market cap of $8.9 billion and a value per token of $513.45.

Litecoin

Litecoin, launched in 2011, was among the first cryptocurrencies to follow in the footsteps of Bitcoin and has often been referred to as "silver to Bitcoin's gold." It was created by Charlie Lee, an MIT graduate and former Google engineer. Litecoin is based on an open-source global payment network that is not controlled by any central authority and uses "scrypt" as a proof of work, which can be decoded with the help of CPUs of consumer-grade. Although Litecoin is like Bitcoin in many ways, it has a faster block generation rate and hence offers a faster transaction confirmation time. Other than developers, there are a growing number of merchants who accept Litecoin. As of January 2021, Litecoin had a market cap of $10.1 billion and a per token value of $153.88, making it the sixth-largest cryptocurrency in the world.

Ethereum

The first Bitcoin alternative on our list, Ethereum, is a decentralized software platform that enables Smart Contracts and Decentralized Applications (DApps) to be built and run without any downtime, fraud, control, or interference from a third party. The goal behind Ethereum is to create a decentralized suite of financial products that anyone in the world can have free access to, regardless of nationality, ethnicity, or faith. This aspect makes the implications for those in some countries more compelling, as those without state infrastructure and state identifications can get access to bank accounts, loans, insurance, or a variety of other financial products.

The applications on Ethereum are run on its platform-specific cryptographic token, ether. Ether is like a vehicle for moving around on the Ethereum platform and is sought by mostly developers looking to develop and run applications inside Ethereum, or now, by investors looking to make purchases of other digital currencies using ether. Ether, launched in 2015, is currently the second-largest digital currency by market cap after Bitcoin, although it lags behind the dominant cryptocurrency by a significant margin. As of January 2021, ether's market cap is roughly 19% of Bitcoin's size.

In 2014, Ethereum launched a pre-sale for ether which received an overwhelming response; this helped to usher in the age of the initial coin offering (ICO). According to Ethereum, it can be used to "codify, decentralize, secure and trade just about anything." Following the attack on the DAO in 2016, Ethereum was split into Ethereum (ETH) and Ethereum Classic (ETC). As of January 2021, Ethereum (ETH) had a market cap of $138.3 billion and a per token value of $1,218.59.

In 2021 Ethereum plans to change its consensus algorithm from proof-of-work to proof-of-stake. This move will allow Ethereum's network to run itself with far less energy as well as improved transaction speed. Proof-of-stake allows network participants to "stake" their ether to the network. This process helps to secure the network and process the transactions that occur. Those who do this are rewarded ether similar to an interest account. This is an alternative to Bitcoin's proof-of-work mechanism where miners are rewarded more Bitcoin for processing transactions.

Polkadot

Polkadot (DOT) is a unique proof-of-stake cryptocurrency that is aimed at delivering interoperability between other blockchains. Its protocol is designed to connect permissioned and permissionless blockchains as well as oracles to allow systems to work together under one roof.

Polkadot's core component is its relay chain that allows the interoperability of varying networks. It also allows for "parachains," or parallel blockchains with their own native tokens for specific use cases.

Where this system differs from Ethereum is that rather than creating just decentralized applications on Polkadot, developers can create their own blockchain while also using the security that Polkadot's chain already has. With Ethereum, developers can create new blockchains but they need to create their own security measures which can leave new and smaller projects open to attack, as the larger a blockchain the more security it has. This concept in Polkadot is known as shared security.

Polkadot was created by Gavin Wood, another member of the core founders of the Ethereum project who had differing opinions on the project's future. As of January 2021, Polkadot has a market capitalization of $11.2 billion and one DOT trades for $12.54.

Ripple

Ripple was founded in 2012 in order to fill a need in the international business market for a fast and efficient way to transfer funds from one country to another. The goal of Ripple is to establish a blockchain that will be used to verify financial transactions. This strategy has the potential to remake the entire global financial system, and the Ripple cryptocurrency also called Ripple but technically named XRP – is an integral part of this goal.

Stellar

Stellar is an open blockchain network designed to provide enterprise solutions by connecting financial institutions for the purpose of large transactions. Huge transactions between banks and investment firms that typically would take several days, a number of intermediaries, and cost a good deal of money, can now be done nearly instantaneously with no intermediaries and cost little to nothing for those making the transaction.

While Stellar has positioned itself as an enterprise blockchain for institutional transactions, it is still an open blockchain that can be used by anyone. The system allows for cross-border transactions between any currencies. Stellar's native currency is Lumens (XLM). The network requires users to hold Lumens to be able to transact on the network.

Stellar was founded by Jed McCaleb, a founding member of Ripple Labs and developer of the Ripple protocol. He eventually left his role with Ripple and went on to co-found the Stellar Development Foundation. Stellar Lumens have a market capitalization of $6.1 billion and are valued at $0.27 as of January 2021.

Cardano

Cardano is an "Ouroboros proof-of-stake" cryptocurrency that was created with a research-based approach by engineers, mathematicians, and cryptography experts. The project was cofounded by Charles Hoskinson, one of the five initial founding members of Ethereum. After having some disagreements with the direction Ethereum was taking, he left and later helped to create Cardano.

The team behind Cardano created its blockchain through extensive experimentation and peer-reviewed research. The researchers behind the project have written over 90 papers on blockchain technology across a range of topics. This research is the backbone of Cardano.

Due to this rigorous process, Cardano seems to stand out among its proof-of-stake peers as well as other large cryptocurrencies. Cardano has also been dubbed the "Ethereum killer" as its blockchain is said to be capable of more. That said, Cardano is still in its early stages. While it has beaten Ethereum to the proof-of-stake consensus model it still has a long way to go in terms of decentralized financial applications.

Cardano aims to be the financial operating system of the world by establishing decentralized financial products similarly to Ethereum as well as providing solutions for chain interoperability, voter fraud, and legal contract tracing, among other things. As of January 2021, Cardano has a market capitalization of $9.8 billion and one ADA trades for $0.31.

Pros and Cons of Altcoins

Here we will discuss some important altcoins, one by one in the sense of their pros and cons.

Bitcoin Cash

Pros: BCH's transaction fees are $0.0019, which is relatively lower than the original Bitcoin having transaction costs $0.20 per transaction. Besides, BCH's transfer time is higher than BTC, so you will not have to wait longer to verify the purchase.

Bitcoin cash has its blockchain technology, and it implements an improved blocksize of 8MB as opposed to blocking the size of

Bitcoin (i.e., 1MB). This limited size increases the transaction fees while lowering transaction speed.

Cons: Due to serious concern regarding centralization in Bitcoin cash, in addition to branding of BCH, it is problematic to distinguish between Bitcoin and Bitcoin Cash.

Bitcoin cash has quite fewer trading pairs as compared to Bitcoin that makes it less tradable among investors. Moreover, another disadvantage of BCH is its low rates of adoption across industries that can impact its growth in the cryptocurrency market.

Litecoin

Pros: As compared to Bitcoin, the transaction speed of Litecoin is four times faster; more precisely, the closing speed of blocks is 10 minutes for Bitcoin, whereas it is just 2.5 minutes for Litecoin. It makes Litecoin less susceptible to attacks. Also, the market cap of LTC is $3.1 Billion.

LTC is relatively stable from other Altcoins as it is based on the Scrypt algorithm. Besides, the transaction fee for LTC is low.

Cons: Investing in Litecoin can be risky as the central authority does not manage it since Bitcoin embraces the SegWit update that takes away one of its unique selling points.

Ethereum (ETH)

Pros: Ethereum is highly secure and accepted by various industries. In the case of Bitcoin crumbles, you can avail Altcoins like Ethereum to fall back on.

ETH has the largest market cap after Bitcoin, and therefore, it can be the best Altcoin to invest. It also carries components like dApps, DAOs (Decentralized Autonomous Organizations), and blockchain smart contracts that make it operative and useful blockchain.

Besides, for executing code on the Ethereum platform, ETH is needed. Since many projects are built on this decentralized platform, ETH can become a potential cryptocurrency in the long run.

Cons: Some do not favor Ethereum due to its scalability issues. For instance, it has a slow transaction time that influences the status and activity of its network. Precisely, the public blockchain of Ethereum can process only 15 to 20 transactions per second as opposed to 45,000 transactions processed by Visa.

Besides, it is highly vulnerable to competition rising in the cryptocurrency market. For instance, other blockchain platforms claim to be more scalable.

Ripple (XRP)

Pros: Ripple network is highly secure and anonymous as opposed to traditional bank services. Adoption rates of XRP are quite high among various financial institutes due to its high traceability and instantaneous transactions.

Cons: Ripple developers decide when and how much XRP coins should be released. Ripple is also vulnerable to attacks once the code is accessible.

Even though Ripple has secured trust and confidence in investors and critical financial institutions, its exercises have low adoption rates.

General Analysis of Altcoins

Advantages

- o Improve on Bitcoin's flaws: Altcoins are generally designed to address a perceived shortcoming with the Bitcoin framework, whether it's speed, mining cost, or some other factor.

- o Provide competition: By tweaking the rules under which Bitcoin operates, altcoin creators make space for new competitors to the Bitcoin system.

- o Low transaction fees: One of the benefits of using altcoins as a payment method, in addition to secure blockchain technology, is the relatively low transaction fees charged for each transaction

Disadvantages

- o Value is very volatile: As an investment, altcoins are very new and their value can change drastically.

o High potential for scams and fraud: Altcoins, as with Bitcoin, are frequently the subject of scams and other fraudulent schemes[21].

Altcoin vs. Bitcoin

Altcoins don't all follow the same rules as Bitcoin. For example, while Bitcoin will only ever mine, or produce, bitcoins every 10 minutes, an altcoin called Litecoin will produce coins every 2.5 minutes. This makes Litecoin able to process payments faster. Litecoin will also produce 84 million litecoins, whereas Bitcoin will only produce 21 million bitcoins[22].

Litecoin also uses a different set of rules for mining than bitcoin. Whereas bitcoins require costly hardware to mine, litecoins can be mined with common computer hardware.

Litecoin is just one of the thousands of altcoins on the market. Some altcoins stand out as popular alternatives to Bitcoin, although they don't reach Bitcoin's $100 billion market cap[23].

Why do differences between cryptocurrencies matter to traders?

The differences between cryptocurrencies matter to traders because they give vital clues as to how supply and demand for each coin may change over time, in turn influencing market prices and how cryptocurrencies are traded.

- o Supply
- o Circulating supply and upper limit

The supply of coins plays an important role in setting market prices. All other things being equal, the scarcer the coin, the more valuable it should be. Bitcoin and bitcoin cash each have an upper limit of 21 million coins, while Litecoin and ripple have expanded maximum supplies of 84 million and 100 billion respectively. These coins will be deflationary once all the coins have been mined or released, while coins like ether – with no fixed limit – have the potential to be inflationary, depending on how much is 'burnt' or lost.

Cryptocurrency mining and release rates

The supply of coins' changes over time as new coins are mined or released. Mining is the process by which 'blocks' of transactions are verified, and new coins released. Bitcoin is currently mined at a rate of 12.5 new coins for every verified block, with the reward halving roughly every four years (the final bitcoins will be mined around the year 2140). Ripple coins, on the other hand, were pre-mined by its founders and are currently being released at a rate of one billion per month.

Despite having fewer applications than many of its newer competitors, Bitcoin's value has soared over the last few years, and it remains the biggest cryptocurrency by market capitalization. This suggests that reputation remains an important factor in cryptocurrency valuations. Press coverage is likely to be an important factor here, with negative press – for example following a major wallet hack – tending to have a negative impact on prices.

Decentralized Applications

While bitcoin, bitcoin cash, and litecoin are standalone cryptocurrencies, ether and ripple exist as part of wider networks with expanded applications. If the popularity of these networks increases or they are adopted by mainstream businesses, demand for their underlying cryptocurrencies could surge.

Transaction speed and scalability

As adoption of cryptocurrencies accelerates, transaction speeds and their ability to handle a high volume of transactions is likely to come under increased scrutiny. Scalability could also be influenced by blockchain size and security, as these factors will affect the profitability of mining, speed of the associated network, and willingness of users to buy and use coins. Traders should therefore pay attention to software updates and forks to see how scaling technology evolves.

CHAPTER 03

Network Security Protocol

Perhaps Bitcoin's greatest technological achievement (and the sine qua non of every altcoin) is building a peer-to-peer transaction system that relies on "cryptographic proof rather than trust" [12]. However, replacing a central authority presents a unique problem with a solution that is not obvious. First, the coin needs to be able to change ownership. Transactions are recorded by combining the digital signatures of each party and a timestamp, so that the transaction date is recorded. This new code represents the coin and its path through the network. This code is then broadcasted to all nodes (computers connected to and running the cryptocurrency network software) on the network. However, it is necessary that the majority of the nodes agree on transactions that have occurred, otherwise double-spending and denial-of-service (DoS) attacks can occur. The mechanism used to reach consensus among nodes puts integrity in the system by verifying that the transaction is indeed legitimate. Hence, transactions are verified, and the system made secure, by implementing certain mechanisms that make it too costly to violate the integrity of the system. Larry Ren, developer of Reddcoin, notes, "The underlying principle of such a mechanism is the necessity of expending resources when confirming transactions" [24]. Various cryptocurrencies have developed novel resources to use as a means of network security. The resource can be a combination of electricity, time, or temporary surrender of coinage, and represents the cost to secure the network. Miners - those who own the underlying resource, and thus expend it - secure the network, and are compensated for their work in the form of either transaction fees or newly minted coins. The mechanism used to secure the network determines the resource chosen and the method used to pay the miners. Thus, the underlying network security mechanism of each coin has a significant impact on the underlying economics of the coin.

Proof of Work

First proposed by Cynthia Dwork and Moni Naor in 1993, "A Proof-of-Work (PoW) is a piece of data which is costly to produce so as to satisfy certain requirements but is trivial to verify" [25]. That is, PoW adds an economic cost to perform a given function. In the case of cryptocurrencies, transactions are not considered verified until a certain amount of energy has been expended. Most altcoins that use the PoW mechanism are direct copies of, or are very similar to, Bitcoin's protocol. The following section will focus on how the mechanism is implemented by Bitcoin.

Hashing Algorithms

In addition to the network security mechanism, hashing algorithms also affect the coin. For PoW mechanisms, the hashing algorithm and the target difficulty of the hash dictate how many hashes - how much energy - is expected to be spent. Because miners are incentivized to find ever more powerful computing equipment, this has created a mining arms race. For instance, mining originally was carried out by CPU (Central Processing Unit); however, the same functions could be carried out by GPU (Graphics Processing Unit) at a much faster rate. GPUs then gave way to Application Specific Integrated Circuits (ASICs), designed to carry out PoW mining at incredible speeds – magnitudes higher than could be done through GPUs. The SHA-256 algorithm used in Bitcoin and various altcoins felt the brunt of this arms race, and many coins have introduced alternative hashing algorithms that are often praised as being ASIC-resistant [26]. However, this is not the case, as ASICs can be designed to carry out any hashing algorithm. It is expensive to do so, so until miners receive enough incentive to build ASICs for a particular hashing algorithm other than SHA-256, like Scrypt, they will likely not. Another problem with this is that economies of scale are created. In order to be decentralized, coins need to have the security distributed among many users. However, small-scale investors no longer see it as profitable to connect their home computers to the coin network, as they would then be forced to compete with much faster ASICs. Hence, this arms race has had the side effect of essentially centralizing network authority into the hands of the largest miners.

Innovation in Cryptocurrency Market

Hashing is a method that involves converting an array of data into a specific code that stores information about this very data. This transformation is called a hash function, and the result of the encryption is called a hash code. Each hash code is unique, and its decryption leads to the receipt of the original data. It is this subspecies of cryptography hashing that is the basis for the formation of cryptocurrency systems, reflecting their essence: the technological nature of creation and the security inherent in these systems. The scheme for obtaining a hash of transactions is shown in the figure below. This technology increases the level of confidentiality and reliability of transaction data. The process of hashing an array of data is as follows: information about the individual operations performed is converted by a hash function, and separate hashes are formed. This encrypted data is combined and modified by the following hash function, and, as a result, the largest combination of functions will be the transaction hash, with which the data will be decrypted.

Furthermore, the hashed data formed in blocks create a single stream of interconnected information, protected using blockchain technology. Due to this, transactions cannot be reversed, and it is impossible to change the degenerated data. Each generated block in the blockchain network contains information about the previous block, including a key a hash function. Information about the network is stored on the computers of all participants simultaneously.

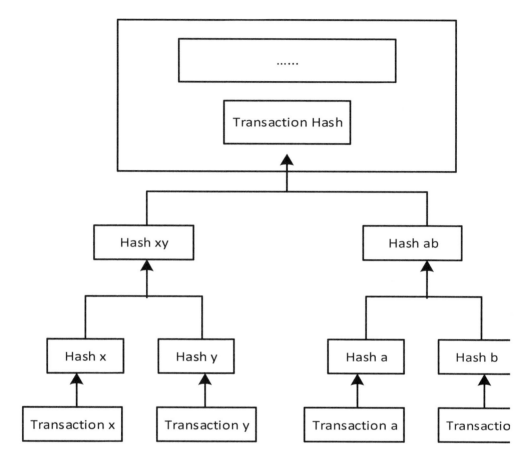

Figure 1: Scheme of obtaining a Hash of Transactions in Cryptocurrencies

Proof of Stake

An alternative to the PoW mechanism is the Proof-of-Stake (PoS) mechanism. Instead of relying on computational power as its "scarce resource," the resource that the network security depends on is ownership of the coin itself – "proof-of-stake means a form of proof-of-ownership" [27]– which is also scarce. Hence, in order to verify a transaction and receive the coin reward (whether new coins or transaction fees), a miner must own some coin himself. Further, the probability that he succeeds in creating a new block is a function of the amount of coin he owns, not of computational power. Hence, there are very little energy costs in this transaction. Further, in order to undermine the integrity of the system, one would have to own more than 50% of the coin currently being staked, in which case violating the coin security would be very costly [27]. Generally, payment takes the form of an "interest" on the amount of coin staked to verify the transaction [10]. Hence, most PoS coins do not have a capped money supply, and are thus inflationary.

However, PoS systems are faced with the challenge of how to initially distribute the coin. Whereas PoW distributes the coins to the miners who add value to the network, a coin that relies purely on PoS must decide whom to distribute the coins to. This can create a host of problems. In fact, most pure PoS coins have turned out to be fraudulent, as the creator often gives himself the majority of the coins [26].

Hybrid PoS-PoW

A hybrid PoW/PoS system uses the PoW mechanism for initial coin minting and distribution. That is, PoW allows the network to distribute new coins to miners. However, over time, the PoS mechanism phases out the PoW mechanism, creating a long-term energy efficient cryptocurrency. Sunny King and Scott Nadal, in their white paper "PPCoin: Peer-to-Peer Crypto-Currency with Proof-of-Stake," are the first to propose and then implement such a hybrid PoW/PoS system. In this hybrid-design, block generation, instead of relying on one CPU per vote, relies on a concept of "coinage" [27]. Coinage is roughly the amount of coin owned multiplied by the life of ownership by the current owner of the coin. Block generation thus goes to the block with the most coinage. Further, coins are minted according to one percent per coin-year consumed, which functions as an interest rate for staking coin [10]. The main advantage, however, is that this system does not rely on high-energy consumption in the long run. Hence, the design is cost-competitive to that which relies on PoW and avoids the distribution problem inherent in PoS.

Byzantine Consensus

Ripple and Stellar offer an alternative security mechanism entirely, which are both implementations of the Byzantine Consensus Protocol [28] [7]. The infrastructure of the coins is that of a distributed network, where each server in the network is faced with the problem of deciding whether other servers in the network are sending accurate messages. The messages in this case are transactions. This system is tolerant of a class of failures known as the Byzantine Generals problem and is thus deemed Byzantine fault tolerant [29]. In the Byzantine Generals problem, the Byzantine army is divided among multiple lieutenants who receive an order of attack or retreat from a commanding general.

However, there are a number of traitors - potentially the commanding general himself yet all loyal generals need to reach consensus despite a small number of traitors working to foil this plan. The problem is that the loyal lieutenants need to reach consensus on which order to obey by sending each other signed messages. Various algorithms have been proposed that provide solutions to the above problem. The distributed networks created by Ripple and Stellar face a problem analogous to the Byzantine Generals problem. First, individuals engaging with one of these coins would have to join a server. Each server in the network is faced with the problem of deciding whether other servers in the network are sending accurate "messages," which in this case are transactions. Ripple's protocol requires that entities join a server. Each server maintains a Unique Node List (UNL), whereby the server only communicates with the nodes on its UNL. This allows servers to be in contact with only trusted servers. Any server can broadcast transactions, and the servers then vote on the transactions. However, servers vote only on transactions that came from other nodes on its UNL. Every few seconds, the servers all send messages back and forth, until the algorithm terminates with consensus or failure to reach consensus. The specific algorithm used in Ripple requires that a transaction be accepted by 80 percent of the servers in order for consensus to be reached. This security mechanism is both much more energy efficient than the PoW mechanism, requires at least an 80% attack on the network in order for the network security to be violated [7].

Mechanism	Decentralized Control	Little Latency	Malleable Trust	Long Run Low Energy Rate
PoW	↑	×	×	×
PoS	↑	↓↑	×	↑
PoS - PoW	↑	↓↑	×	↑

Table 1: Summary of Each Mechanism

CHAPTER 04

Cryptocurrency as New Legal Phenomenon

Nowadays, the majority of crypto-asset operations are outside the legal field, which is good to some extent, because no one interferes with them. On the other hand, there are risks, of course. In particular, state financial monitoring and control is impossible. This is really undesirable because not all operations related to crypto assets activities are positive. There is a danger of using cryptocurrencies in transactions that are beyond the law. And it is necessary to create protection against such actions. Participants of the crypto market wait from the state not regulation, which is perceived by the IT sector as an unwanted interference but defying legal status. Under such conditions, legal aspects of certain types of legal liability for violations in the field of cryptocurrency become of particular relevance[30].

The definition of cryptocurrency as a commodity means that transactions on its sales are to be taxed on the added value. The exchange of cryptocurrency for goods falls under the legal regulation of barter transactions. If cryptocurrency is recognized as a security or other financial instrument, then the activity of cryptocurrency exchanges, similar to stock exchanges, must be licensed by the state. Thus, the definition of the legal nature of cryptocurrency as the basis of its legal status is a priority task that must be solved by the state before any measures are taken to legalize cryptocurrencies[31].

Legal Nature of Cryptocurrency in Different States

To date, most countries in the world are trying to regulate the cryptocurrency relations and settle them, focusing mainly on the issues related to licensing operations with cryptocurrencies, taxation, as well as countering the legalization of proceeds from criminal transactions and financing of terrorism. At the same time, state authorities often fail to have a clear position on the legal nature of cryptocurrency, and therefore, try to regulate its turnover "blindly." As S. A. Timofeev notes, attempts to somehow regulate legal relations related to cryptocurrency are meaningless until digital rights, money and contracts become objects of civil rights [32].

In most cases, cryptocurrency is defined as one of the known and regulated objects of civil turnover. Thus, the Australian Taxation Office (ATO) has decided that the digital currency is a commodity, not a currency, which corresponds to the tax instructions provided by the relevant authorities in other countries, such as Canada and Singapore. Resolutions of ATO of December 17, 2014, stipulate that transactions in bitcoins are an analog to a barter agreement and have similar tax consequences. ATO also notes that bitcoin is neither money nor foreign currency, and for taxation purposes, the sale of bitcoin is not considered as a financial service. According to the Australian Securities and Investments Commission (ASIC), the digital currencies themselves are not included in the legal definition of a "financial product", and the digital currency trading does not fall under the category of financial services [33]. A different point of view was expressed by Stephen Poloz, the Governor of the

Central Bank of Canada, who stated in January 2018 that he objected to the term "cryptocurrencies", since they are not currencies, they are not assets, they can rather technically be classified as securities [34].

For a long time, Russia had no clear position of the state regarding the legal nature of cryptocurrency and its legal status. Despite the fact that there is no direct ban on cryptocurrency transactions, in most cases, the officials' statements and the positions of government bodies showed a very cautious approach to the potential permission of settlements in cryptocurrency in the Russian Federation. The Bank of Russia considered it premature to let cryptocurrencies, as well as any financial instruments nominated or associated with cryptocurrencies, circulate and be used at organized trades and in settlement and clearing infrastructure on the territory of the Russian Federation for servicing deals with cryptocurrencies and their derivatives [35]. The Federal Tax Service of Russia stated that transactions related to the acquisition or sale of cryptocurrency using foreign exchange values (foreign currency and external securities) and/or currency of the Russian Federation are currency transactions [36], thus equating cryptocurrency with the foreign currency. To date, they have drafted and discussed a federal law "On Digital Financial Assets", which attributes cryptocurrency to property in electronic form, created with the use of cryptographic means. In accordance with the draft law, cryptocurrency is not recognized as a legitimate means of payment in the territory of the Russian Federation [37].

One of the options for determining the legal nature of cryptocurrency, which has been repeatedly proposed by officials of different countries, including Russia, is the introduction of the concept of a "digital commodity" ("virtual commodity"). With this variant accepted, the civil legislation should be added with norms about a new object of the civil rights - a digital (virtual) thing. However, the extension of the real rights regime to such an object is difficult since it is intangible. From the point of view of the civil law, only a tangible thing can be alienated, whereas intangible objects of civil rights, including the results of intellectual activity and the means of individualization of legal persons, goods, works, services and enterprises, are not transferable, i. e. only the rights on them are subject to alienation.

A number of states did gradually come to understanding that equating cryptocurrency with the already existing objects of civil circulation is not right. In February 2016, in the UK, the Commonwealth Working Group on Virtual Currencies published a report on the legal status of the digital currency and the regulation of transactions in it, which adopted the virtual currency definition proposed by the Financial Action Task Force (FATF), a group for combating money laundering: a digital representation of value that can be digitally traded and functions as a medium of exchange, a unit of account and/or a stored value, but does not have legal tender status in any jurisdiction [9]. We believe that this definition most accurately reveals the essence of cryptocurrency and expresses a specific position regarding its functions as a means of accumulation, while excluding its use as a means of payment.

Legal Regulation Issues

It is common knowledge that financial law depends on policy and its significant manifestations. M.V. Karaseva argues that financial law, like any other branch of law, is a political phenomenon. Furthermore, she specifies that policy is obligatory for the formation of any regulations. Law is the most effective guide to the policy. She argues that there are no apolitical branches of law from the perspective of forming regulations and implementing present policies. By nature, financial policy is a type of state policy. Here we are going to review the legal and policy landscape surrounding cryptocurrencies *around the World*.

Under the National Constitution of **Argentina** the only authority capable of issuing legal currency is the Central Bank. [38] Bitcoins are not legal currency strictly speaking, since they are not issued by the government monetary authority and are not legal tender.

Belize does not appear to have any legislation that specifically regulates cryptocurrencies. [21]Trading businesses in Belize are regulated by the International Financial Services Commission of Belize.

Bermuda does not have legislation or regulations that specifically govern cryptocurrencies. The government is, however, in the early stages of crafting legislation and regulations that aim to establish Bermuda as an international destination for digital currencies, similar to its position in the insurance and reinsurance sectors.

The use of virtual currencies is prohibited in **Bolivia**. The Central Bank has stated that the use of currency not issued by the monetary authority is not allowed in the country. Cryptocurrencies such as Bitcoin are not regulated and therefore, the Central Bank warns about the possible losses that people using them are exposed to.

On November 16, 2017, the **Brazilian** Federal Reserve Bank (Banco Central do Brasil) issued Notice No. 31,379 alerting citizens to the risks arising from the custody and trading operations of virtual currencies.

Canada allows the use of cryptocurrencies, including Bitcoin. According to a Financial Consumer Agency of Canada webpage on digital currencies, "you can use digital currencies to buy goods and services on the Internet and in stores that accept digital currencies. You may also buy and sell digital currency on open exchanges, called digital currency or cryptocurrency exchanges." However, cryptocurrencies, including Bitcoin, are not considered legal tender in Canada; "only the Canadian dollar is considered official currency in Canada."

The President of the European Central Bank (ECB), Mario Draghi, warned that bitcoin and other digital currencies are "very risky assets" due to their high volatility and speculative prices. He stated that "digital currencies are not subject to a specific supervisory approach," but that "work is under way in the Single Supervisory Mechanism to identify potential prudential risks that these digital assets could pose to supervised institutions."

Cryptocurrencies remain largely unregulated in France, with two ordinances on blockchain technology being the only legislative action taken so far. However, the French government is actively moving towards establishing a regulatory regime.

A draft law on digital financial assets was published by the Ministry of Finances on January 20, 2018, and introduced in the State Duma on March 20, 2018. The bill defines "mining" as activities aimed at the creation of cryptocurrency with the purpose of receiving compensation in the form of cryptocurrency. Mining is treated as an entrepreneurial activity subject to taxation if the miner exceeds the energy consumption limits established by the government for three months in a row. As to initial coin offerings (ICO), only qualified investors are allowed to participate in them, except for cases to be defined by the Central Bank.

The Central Bank of **Iran** (CBI) officially announced on April 22, 2018, that it has prohibited the handling of cryptocurrencies by all Iranian financial institutions, including banks and credit institutions. The decision also bans currency exchanges from buying and selling virtual currencies or adopting measures to facilitate or promote them.

The **Saudi Arabian** Monetary Agency (SAMA) has issued a warning against bitcoin because it is not being monitored or supported by any legitimate financial authority.

In December 2014 the **South African** Reserve Bank (SARB), the central banking institution whose responsibilities include formulating and implementing monetary policy and issuing banknotes and coins in the country, issued a position paper on virtual currencies.

The government of **India** stated in early 2018 that cryptocurrencies such as bitcoin are not legal tender in India.

In **Japan**, cryptocurrency exchange businesses are regulated. The Payment Services Act was amended in June 2016 and the amendment took effect on April 1, 2017.

Chinese regulators are not recognizing virtual currencies such as bitcoin as a tool for retail payments like paper bills, coins, or credit cards. The banking system is not accepting any existing virtual currencies or providing relevant services.

The legal regulation of the relations connected with the issuance and turnover of cryptocurrencies should be preceded by understanding of the economic nature and legal nature of cryptocurrency based on its key characteristics and functions, as well as the legislative definition of cryptocurrency (virtual money) and its legal status.

The absence of legal regulation on cryptocurrency complicates protecting the rights of cryptocurrency holders in the courts. According to some court decisions, Bitcoin has not been recognized as goods or property rights to the entries in the open database of Blockchain and determined as an object that cannot be subject to legal protection at all and cannot be claimed by enforcement.

Cryptocurrency Scams

Fraudulent cryptocurrency offerings have taken their place alongside imaginary gas and oil wells, fabricated promissory notes and overseas investments, among others, as the basis for a new raft of scams. The allure of cryptocurrency-related scams relies on the same hooks as more traditional schemes: get in on the ground floor, don't miss out, there's no real risk, you're guaranteed high returns, and why settle for low returns when you could be earning so much more.

Another problem is that fraudsters use the Internet to give themselves an air of legitimacy. Anyone can set up a professional-looking online presence that appears to portray highly skilled experts and flashy facilities. As an investor, though, it's hard to know who is really being depicted in those images[38].

CHAPTER 05

Improvement

It is undeniable that the emergence of cryptocurrency will play a significant role in the world's economic fabric. It is the fact that every economist, researchers, investors alike has to act and considerable measures to strengthen their knowledge on the blockchain technology in general[39]. As cryptocurrency has not yet reached maturity in term of time frame, further studies on its technology, potential and risk should be studied to ensure that the opportunities are not just a mere fluke. Also, the upcoming challenges do not mitigate stakeholders into the doldrums of financial failures.

Future Work on Cryptocurrencies

Future research on reducing the 51% attack on the blockchain mining network should be further enhanced [40]. The security protocol should be better, if not the same than the conventional centralized banking system in protecting the customer's monetary assets. Security aspect of users warrants the ground-breaking testimonial from the players in this new industry so that the confidence and trust of the blockchain technology would allow it to be the norm for users in doing their daily transaction via the internet. In reducing the cost of mining the currency, a proof of stake would provide lesser energy consumption in mining these digital coins [41]. In proof of stake methodology, a person needs to validate the coins that they own and the amount possessed. The person needs to create a transaction of their coins that they send to their account as a reward with the information of predefined percentage. The proof of stake resembles a raffle-like scheme that provide the same chance for all miners. Furthermore, a hybrid method that consists of both proof of work and proof of stake had been suggested, by rewarding fraction of the proof of work to all nodes that are active and at the same time the stake determines the ticket gained to all raffle.[42] suggested Proof of Activity (PoA), that combines the proof of work and proof of stake. In PoA, the activity term refers to active users that maintain the full online node and the one that should be rewarded. Contrarily, in proof of stake, offline users can still accumulate the coins over time and this can lead to double spending of the same block. PoA provides much better security in facing future threat on the cryptocurrency. It has a bigger storage space and the network communication permits low penalty. Plus, PoA also has low transaction fees, consuming less energy and the topology of the network can be improvised. Thus, PoA alternative serve as a better platform for cryptocurrency due to its ability to fend of double spending and most importantly the cost in acquiring the cryptocurrency compared to proof of work. The market has been plunged with many new cryptocurrencies that had already made it into the market and there are many still waiting to be released. There have been many emerging currencies that are challenging and competing Bitcoin in term of its price and market capitalization. Even though at the time of writing, only Ethereum and Ripple had reached three figure prices. [38] proposed a model called Moran process on new emerging cryptocurrency. The model does simulation on the market where the currencies are traded. The model is able to simulate the constant rate of new mined coins, trading activities of the agents and the communication among users trading on the markets[43]. All the currencies are interchangeable among themselves, with the acknowledgement of the account holders. It was also found that Bitcoin can be traded with other coins and the future might see that the highly warranted Bitcoin be replaced by other fascinating coins that may have better features. Therefore, studying on these features such as security, return on investment and low mining cost can determine which of the new and emerging digital coin can replace Bitcoin in the near futures.

Future-work on using proof of work has been discussed in [43]. One of it is to maximize the byproduct of the proof of work by reusing it. Reusing this byproduct in the sense that the resource in solving any mathematical puzzle by an already awarded user can reuse it by rewarding other user from the formulated solved problem. Another suggestion is to use the energy generated by the mining process from electrical energy to heat energy. This can be realized in cold climate countries, where the substantially high heat energy released from the computation of solving the mathematical puzzle can be used to heat residential houses and other household chores requiring heat energy.

It is realized that having considerable knowledge in the blockchain technology would be essential in controlling the negative impact of using cryptocurrency in day-to-day activities[38]. Hence, expertise in this field should collaborate with policy makers and the government agencies in making regulations and policies pertaining to a country's stand in using cryptocurrency. Knowledge management among industry players and researchers should be enhanced to make the people understand the potential and risk in using cryptocurrency. Even experts from the institution of higher learning should be engaged with the public as they have the knowledge resource that facilitating the community in having better

knowledge on certain issues [44].

CONCLUSION

Cryptocurrencies are here to stopover. Future of trading lies well with new emerging technologies that are able to benefit mankind. The cryptocurrency industry is speedily moving forward. It has shown itself to be resilient in the face of major thefts, including government shutdowns. This paper has reviewed the opportunities in cryptocurrency in term of its security of its technology, low transaction cost and high investment return. Improvement and future work on cryptocurrency include improving the security protocol, working on proof of activity, using the byproduct of proof of work and applying the knowledge management system. Additionally, the industry has expanded dramatically in the number of coins currently in circulation. Industry has also shown its creativity in implementing workable solutions to deficiencies in the development of new coins. Bitcoin may not dominate the industry in the long run, but the industry owes its existence to the pioneering anarchic coin.

References

[1] & S. Ali, R., Barrdear, J., Clews, R., "The economics of digital currencies.," *J.*, no. Bank of England Quarterly Bulletin, pp. 276–286.

[2] A. Nakamoto, S., & Bitcoin, "A peer-to-peer electronic cash system.," *Bitcoin. Retrieved.*

[3] T. Böhme, R., Christin, N., Edelman, B., & Moore,

"Bitcoin: Economics, technology, and governance.," *J. Econ. Perspect.*, pp. 213–238, 2015.

[4]   G. (2015). Kiayias, A., & Panagiotakos, "Speed-Security Tradeoff in Blockchain Protocols.," *IACR Cryptol. ePrint Arch. 2015, 1019.*

[5]   S. Nakamoto, "A Peer-to-Peer Electronic Cash System," *Bitcoin:*, 2008.

[6]   "Crypto-Currency Market Capitalizations," *[Online].*

[7]   and A. B. David Schwartz, Noah Youngs, "'The Ripple Protocol Consensus Algorithm,'" *Ripple Labs Inc,.*

[8]   S. N. S. King., "Peer-to-Peer Crypto-Currency with Proof-of-Stake.," *PPCoin:*, no. [Online].

[9]   J. Lee., "No Title," *Nu. [Online].*

[10]   R. Farell, "An Analysis of the Cryptocurrency Industry," *Whart. Res. Sch. Journal. Pap.*, vol. 130, no. 5, pp. 1–23, 2015.

[11]   R. A. Radford, "The economic organisation of a POW camp. Economica," pp. 189–201, 1945.

[12]   S. Nakamoto., "Bitcoin: A Peer-to-Peer Electronic Cash System.," no. [Online].

[13]   B. Chappell., "No Title," *npr. [Online].*

[14]   P. Rizzo., "No Title," *CoinDesk. [Online].*

[15]   M. ANDREESSEN, "No Title," *New York Times. [Online].*

[16]   R. P. Dos Santos, "On the Philosophy of Bitcoin/Blockchain Technology: Is it a Chaotic, Complex System?," *Metaphilosophy*, vol. 48, no. 5, p. 620–633.

[17]   C. Kethineni, S., Cao, Y., & Dodge, "Use of Bitcoin in Darknet Markets: Examining Facilitative Factors on BitcoinRelated Crimes.," *Am. J. Crim. Justice*, vol. 43(2), no. DOI 10.1007/s12103-017-9394-6, pp. 141–157, 2017.

[18]   D. O'Dwyer, K. J., & Malone, "Bitcoin mining and its energy footprint.," *25th IET Irish Signals Syst. Conf. China-*

irel. Int. Conf. Inf. Commun. Technol. (ISSC/CIICT 2014)., no. Limerick, Ireland., pp. 26–27, 2014.

[19] "Crypto-Currency Market Capitalizations.," no. [Online].

[20] "'How Does Bitcoin Work?,'" *Bitcoin.org.*

[21] "'Cryptocurrency Scams.,'" *Texas State Secur. Board.*

[22] "'What Is Litecoin?,'" *Litecoin.org.*

[23] "'Economic and Non-Economic Trading In Bitcoin: Exploring the Real Spot Market For The World's First Digital Commodity,'" *SEC.gov.*, p. 5, 2020.

[24] "Blockchain info.," no. [online].

[25] C. D. and M. Naor, "No Title," 1993.

[26] L. Ren, "'Proof of Stake Velocity: Building the Social Currency of the Digital Age,'" 2010.

[27] S. N. S. King., "Peer-to-Peer Crypto-Currency with Proof-of-Stake.," no. [online], 2012.

[28] D. Mazières., "A Federated Model for Internet-level Consensus.," *Stellar Consens. Protoc.*, no. [online], 2015.

[29] and M. P. Leslie Lamport, Robert Shostak, "'The Byzantine Generals Problem,'" *ACM Trans. Program. Lang. Syst.*, pp. 382–401, 1982.

[30] Y. L. 1. Oleksii Drozd, "Ruslan Serbin THEORETICAL AND LEGAL PERSPECTIVE ON CERTAIN TYPES OF LEGAL LIABILITY IN CRYPTOCURRENCY RELATION," vol. 3, 2017.

[31] O S Bolotaeva et al, "'The Legal Nature of Cryptocurrency':," *IOP Conf. Ser. Earth Environ.*, no. Sci. 272 032166., 2019.

[32] "Timofeev S A An attempt to legalize cryptocurrencies: will the state dare? [Electronic resource]."

[33] "Digital currency-game changer or bit player Parliament of Australia."

[34] "The positions of the world countries on regulating

cryptocurrencies as of February 2018."

[35] "On the use of private 'virtual currencies'
(cryptocurrencies)"," *imformation Bank Russ. 04 Sept. 2017*
", no. Consultant.ru legal reference system, 2017.

[36] "On the measures of controlling cryptocurrency turnover
Letter of the Federal Tax Service of Russia of 03 October
2016 #OA-18-17/1027 Consultant.ru legal reference
system."

[37] "'On digital financial assets,'" *(in Ed. Submitt. to State
Duma, State Assem. RF, text as 20 March 2018)*, vol. Draft
of t, no. Consultant.ru legal reference system.

[38] M. A. Fauzi, N. Paiman, and Z. Othman, "Bitcoin and
cryptocurrency: Challenges, opportunities and future
works," *J. Asian Financ. Econ. Bus.*, vol. 7, no. 8, pp. 695–
704, 2020.

[39] T. Fauzi, M. A., Tan, C. N. L., & Ramayah, "Knowledge
sharing intention at Malaysian higher learning institutions:

The academics'," *viewpoint. Knowl. Manag. E-Learning An Int. Journal,* vol. 10(2), pp. 163–176, 2018.

[40] N. Shi, "A new proof-of-work mechanism for bitcoin.," *Financ. Innov.,* vol. 2(1), no. DOI 10.1186/s40854-016-0045-6, p. 31.

[41] H. (2017). Vranken, "Sustainability of bitcoin and blockchains.," *Curr. Opin. Environ. Sustain.,* pp. 1–9.

[42] M. Bentov, I., Lee, C., Mizrahi, A., & Rosenfeld, "Proof of Activity: Extending Bitcoin's Proof of Work via Proof of Stake.," *ACM SIGMETRICS Perform. Eval. Rev. 42(3),* pp. 34–37, 2014.

[43] M. Cocco, L., Concas, G., & Marchesi, "Using an artifiial fiancial market for studying a cryptocurrency market," *ournal Econ. Interact. Coord. 12(2),* no. DOI 10.1007/s11403-015-0168-2, pp. 345–365.

[44] A. O. Fauzi, M. A., Nya-Ling, C. T., Thurasamy, R., & Ojo, "An integrative model of knowledge sharing in Malaysian

higher learning institute."